BUGS
for
LUNCH

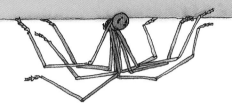

For my adventurous friend Barbara Lucas,
who would not hesitate to eat a well-cooked bug
—M.F.

To my son Matthew, who has always been fascinated by bugs
—S.L.

Text copyright © 1999 by Margery Facklam
Illustrations copyright © 1999 by Sylvia Long

Published by Charlesbridge
85 Main Street, Watertown, MA 02472
(617) 926-0329 • www.charlesbridge.com

Library of Congress Cataloging-in-Publication Data
Facklam, Margery.
  Bugs for lunch/Margery Facklam; illustrated by Sylvia Long.
    p.   cm.
Summary: Rhyming text introduces bug-eating animals
such as geckos, trout, or even people. Includes additional
facts about each creature.
  ISBN-13: 978-0-88106-271-7 (reinforced for library use)
  ISBN-10: 0-88106-271-5 (reinforced for library use)
  ISBN-13: 978-0-88106-272-4 (softcover)
  ISBN-10: 0-88106-272-3 (softcover)
  1. Animals—Food—Juvenile literature. 2. Edible insects—
Juvenile literature. [1. Animals—Food habits. 2. Edible
insects.] I. Long, Sylvia, ill. II. Title.
QL756.5.F33   1999
591.5'3—dc21   98-4640

Printed in Korea
(hc) 10 9 8 7 6 5 4 3 2
(sc) 20 19 18 17 16 15

The illustrations in this book were done in pen and ink and
  Winsor and Newton watercolors on Winsor and Newton
  artist's watercolor paper, 140-pound hot-pressed.
The display type and text type were set in Giovanni.
Color separations were made by Pre-Press Company, Inc.,
  East Bridgewater, Massachusetts
Printed April 2013 by Sung In Printing in Gunpo-Si,
  Kyonggi-Do, Korea
Production supervision by Brian G. Walker
Designed by Diane M. Earley

Everyone uses the nickname "bugs" for all kinds of
insects, spiders, and other crawly things. There is only
one group of insects that scientists consider "true
bugs," such as mealy bugs, squash bugs, and others.

With thanks for generous assistance with
illustration references to Peter Menzel and
MAN EATING BUGS: The Art & Science of Eating Insects
by Peter Menzel and Faith D'Aluisio
A Material World Book
Distributed by Ten Speed Press, Berkeley, CA
1998

BUGS
for
LUNCH

Margery Facklam
Illustrated by Sylvia Long

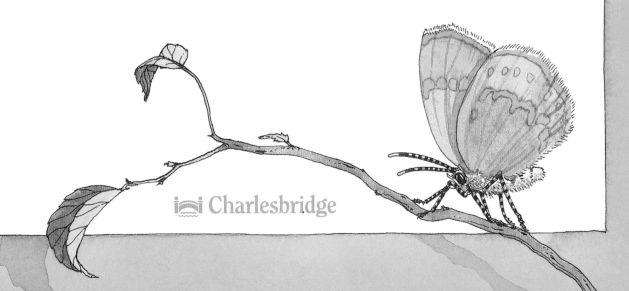

Charlesbridge

If your lunch was a bug,
Who could you be?
Maybe a nuthatch
At work in a tree,

Or maybe a spider
Trapping a fly,

Or a bat catching bugs
As it cruises the sky.

You might be a gecko

Or maybe a mouse,
Eating the insects
In somebody's house.

You might be a shrew,
Not just eating lunch,
But snacking all day
On bugs by the bunch.

You could be a toad,
Zapping a fly
With a flip of the tongue
In the blink of an eye;

Or maybe a mantis
Ready to prey
On any size insect
That happens its way.

You might be a trout,
At home in a brook,
Looking for insects
That aren't on a hook.

You could be a bear
Searching for honey,
But finding that bees
Taste just as yummy.

Or maybe an aardvark,
Whose tongue, long and sticky,
Slurps termites and ants
That others think icky.

You could be a plant
That can't chase a fly,
But just sits and waits
For its food to drop by.

If your lunch was a bug,
You might be just you,

Munching on insects
As some people do.

More About Bugs for Lunch

There are more insects in the world than any other kind of animal. More than 800,000 insects have been studied and named, but scientists believe that there are probably millions that nobody knows about yet. It's a good thing that insects are food for so many creatures, or the world might be overrun with them.

The *NUTHATCH* is called the upside-down bird because it walks headfirst down tree trunks as it searches for food. With its strong beak, it pries out insects, caterpillars, and insect eggs that are hidden in cracks in the bark.

SPIDERS catch insects in webs and traps made of silk. Each species of spider has a distinctive design for its web or trap. When they catch more than they can eat at one time, most spiders wrap the leftovers in silk to save for a later meal.

BATS fly from their roosts to look for food as the sun goes down. But even in total darkness, they can catch insects. Bats send out a constant stream of sounds that are pitched so high that people cannot hear them. As these sounds hit objects, they echo back to the bat. When an insect flies across this beam of sound, the bat can tell exactly where the bug is and can swoop down to catch it in flight.

A *GECKO* is a small lizard that lives in warm climates. Many people like to have geckos in their gardens and backyards. They know that geckos will come out of hiding at night to eat moths and other insects that people find pesky.

Not everyone likes to have a *MOUSE* in the house because mice nibble on almost anything they can find. Perhaps if more people knew that mice also eat juicy beetle grubs, insect eggs, and moths, they wouldn't mind having a few mice around.

A *SHREW* is one the smallest mammals in the world, and probably one of the busiest. Between short naps, shrews are always on the run, searching for insects. They use so much energy that they cannot go more than a few hours without eating. Every day they eat enough insects to equal two or three times their own weight.

If you find a *TOAD* in your garden, don't chase it away—it's a champion insect eater! A toad's long, sticky tongue is fastened to the front edge of its lower jaw. When a toad sees a bug, it shoots out its tongue, zaps the insect, and has eaten it before you can blink an eye.

A *PRAYING MANTIS* can sit as still as a twig on a tree for hours. When a juicy bug lands nearby, the mantis lashes out and grabs the insect with its spiny front legs. Mantises are welcome in gardens because they eat so many destructive insects. The praying mantis got its name because when it holds its front legs together in front of its face, it looks like it is praying.

When a *TROUT* spots an insect cruising above a brook, it will leap from the cold, clear water and catch the insect in flight. Fishermen often bait their hooks with artificial flies they have made to look like the mayflies and other insects they know trout like to eat.

BEARS aren't fussy eaters. They like all kinds of food—fish, berries, mice, insects, and insect grubs—but they really love honey. When a bear climbs a tree and tears into a beehive with its long claws, bees swarm out. But the bear doesn't seem to mind. Its thick fur protects it from bee stings while it munches juicy bees mixed with the yummy honey.

AARDVARKS, or "earth pigs," live in deep burrows in Africa. They come out of their tunnels at night, when warthogs and their other enemies are sleeping. After an aardvark digs open a huge termite hill or ant nest, it slurps up the swarming insects with its long, sticky tongue.

The **VENUS FLYTRAP** is a carnivorous, or meat-eating, plant. Its hinged leaves are edged with spiny teeth. The slight pressure of an insect landing on a few sensitive hairs on the leaf triggers the leaf to snap shut. In a few days, after the trapped insect has been digested, the leaf opens, ready for another meal to land.

YOU might eat insects, too, especially if you live in a country where meat is scarce. In Cambodia a fat, roasted tarantula is a treat. People who live in central Australia gather moth caterpillars called witchetty grubs to roast in the ashes and hot sand around a campfire. And in Indonesia children use flexible reeds covered with sticky sap to catch dragonflies for a delicious stir-fry served on rice.